CHOSEN

CALLED

KEPT

CHOSEN
CALLED
KEPT

The Conclusions of the Synod of Dort

Translated and arranged
for prayerful reflection and study

by C.W.H. Griffiths, M.A.

pearlpublications.co.uk
Contact: info@pearlpublications.co.uk
CHOSEN – CALLED – KEPT: The Conclusions of the Synod of Dort translated and arranged for prayerful reflection and study

---

The moral rights of the author of this book have been asserted.
All rights reserved. Copyright © 2022 by C.W.H. Griffiths.

No part of this publication may be reproduced or transmitted in any form or by any means without acknowledgement. The typographical presentation of the text may not be reproduced without written permission from the author.

If any rights have been inadvertently infringed, the publisher apologises and asks that the omission be excused. Pearl Publications undertakes to correct any such unintentional oversight in subsequent printings.

1. Synod of Dort (1618-1619). 2. Reformed Church – Creeds.
3. Reformed Church - Doctrines.

First published in this form 2022.
ISBN 978-1-901397-01-7 (Paperback).
ISBN 978-1-901397-02-4 (Hardback).

Cover design: David W. Legg.

About the Author

Chris Griffiths is a former pastor and college lecturer. 'Our Griffiths family is a testimony to God's faithfulness to his covenant promises over at least five generations' (Ps. 103:17).

Acknowledgement

My gratitude is expressed to the Afrikaans Christians to whom I ministered in 2008, and through whom I came to treasure and delight in this wonderful statement of God's saving grace.

CONTENTS

What was the Synod of Dort? 1

What is special about this Edition? 5

How to use this Book 7

Opening Prayer 8

Weekly arrangement for using these Articles 9

Part 1 Unconditional Election 13

Part 2 Particular Redemption (or Limited Atonement) 35

Parts 3 and 4 Total Depravity and Irresistible Grace 45

Part 5 The Perseverance of the Elect 67

Glossary 85

Further Reading 91

Endnotes 93

Upcoming books by Pearl Publications 95

WHAT WAS THE SYNOD OF DORT?

The Decision of the Synod of Dort on the Five Main Points of Doctrine in Dispute in the Netherlands is known as the 'Canons of Dort'. A 'canon' is a formal decree of a Church Council that gives rules of faith or practice. The title of this book uses the more easily understood word 'conclusions' instead of 'canons'. This statement of doctrine was developed and approved by the great Synod that met in the city of Dort (Dordt or Dordrecht) in Holland in 1618-1619.

Although it was a national synod of the Reformed Churches of the Netherlands, it was an international event. Not only were there sixty-two Dutch delegates, there were also twenty-seven foreign delegates representing eight countries or regions[1]. Philip Schaff[2] wrote, 'The Synod of Dort is the only synod of a quasi-Ecumenical character in the history of the Reformed Churches. In this respect it is even more important than the Westminster Assembly of Divines, which was confined to England and Scotland'. It was the consensus of all the Reformed churches concerning the salvation of sinners. All the delegates had voting powers.

---

[1] As Samuel Miller notes (Preface to Thomas Scott's *Articles of the Synod of Dort*), the Church of England sent four delegates as it considered itself, and was considered at that time, a Protestant and Reformed Church. Lutherans were not present.
[2] Philip Schaff, *The Creeds of Christendom*.

Professor Smeaton, one of the founding fathers of the Free Church of Scotland, wrote, 'Representatives were invited from all the Reformed Churches, and these deputies eagerly came to that great Council, except where the Governments, from jealousy, refused permission to attend, which was the case with France[1]. All the topics were discussed with fairness, erudition, and zeal for truth. This great Synod, equal in importance to any of the Ecumenical Councils, is the glory of the Reformed Church. Since the first Four General Councils, none have ever assembled with a more momentous charge or commission. It gave forth in its decrees a full and all-sided outline of the doctrines of special grace; and nobly was its work discharged. The decrees of the Synod were not only made the fundamental Articles of the Dutch Church, but continue, as part of the literature of these questions, to have a significance for all time, and it may be questioned whether anything more valuable as an ecclesiastical testimony for the doctrines of sovereign, special, efficacious grace was ever prepared on this important theme since the days of the Apostles. Its great point was to show that the Spirit produces all, and man acts all. Nowhere has the renewing work of the Holy Spirit been more correctly and fully exhibited than in the Canons of the Synod of Dort'.[2] When he left

---

[1] The seats for the French Huguenots were left empty during the Council. The French Reformed Church adopted the Canons of Dort the following year.
[2] George Smeaton, *The Doctrine of the Holy Spirit*.

the Synod, Bishop Joseph Hall, one of the English delegates, declared, 'There was no place on earth so like heaven as the Synod of Dort'[1].

The Synod of Dort was called to settle a serious controversy in the Dutch churches caused by the rise of Arminianism. Jacob Arminius (1560-1609), a theological professor at Leiden University, questioned the Church's teaching on salvation. In 1610, after his death, forty-three of his followers presented their 'Remonstrance'[2] to the Dutch Government, setting out their views.

The Arminians taught:
> (1) God chose or 'elected' those who he knew in advance would have faith.
> (2) The death of Christ was for everyone (virtually not actually).
> (3) Man has free will to choose (therefore his moral depravity is only partial).
> (4) Man can resist and reject God's calling.
> (5) A converted man or woman can lose their salvation.

They wanted the Reformed doctrinal standards to be revised and their own views protected by the Government so that they could remain in the state Church. The conflict became so severe that it led the Netherlands to the brink of civil war. Finally, in 1617, the Government called this national Synod to settle the issues.

---

[1] Quoted by Samuel Miller in his Preface to Thomas Scott's *Articles of the Synod of Dort*.
[2] They were therefore known as 'the Remonstrants'.

The Synod held 154 sessions over seven months (November 1618 to May 1619). Thirteen Remonstrant theologians unsuccessfully tried various tactics to delay the work of Synod and to divide the delegates. They were eventually excluded and the Synod worked on the debated points, giving what are now popularly called 'the five points of Calvinism'. Although these 'five points' do not give the full scope of 'Calvinism', they certainly lie at the heart of the Reformed faith. They flow from the principle 'it is God who saves'. They have been given the mnemonic TULIP: <u>T</u>otal Depravity; <u>U</u>nconditional Election; <u>L</u>imited Atonement; <u>I</u>rresistible Grace; <u>P</u>erseverance of the Elect. However, the sequence of the Articles follows that of the 'Remonstrance' and therefore differs from the mnemonic (it is rather 'ULTIP').

The statement of doctrine was divided into four parts. The third and fourth (Total Depravity and Irresistible Grace) were combined into one. The delegates at Dort considered them to be inseparable.

The Synod declared that this statement of faith is 'in agreement with the Word of God and accepted till now in the Reformed Churches'. It is important to note that the Synod was not re-interpreting or creating doctrine. The Arminian doctrines were the innovation. This was the reply.

WHAT IS SPECIAL ABOUT THIS EDITION?

Unlike the Westminster standards, the language of which was English[1], the Synod used Latin – the international language of the day. Its statements are often long and finely balanced sentences. It arose from a controversy, and it was important to make precise statements. Parts of it therefore read like a legal document in the original. One sentence in Thomas Scott's translation runs to 50 lines. However, putting the Confession into contemporary English with shorter sentences would lose the meaning, the force, and fullness of its statements.

1. We have therefore arranged the text on the page in a way that keeps the structure, but makes the meaning clearer to the modern reader. The forceful statements and comparisons can be seen more clearly as line after line expands and develops God's way of salvation.
2. We have endeavoured to make the translation as close to the original as possible, but have tried to avoid unnecessary 'latinisms'.
3. We have included a glossary to explain some of the key words used in the Latin. There is benefit in thinking about their fuller meaning. Words underlined in the text are in the glossary.
4. We have added summary sub-headings to each of the Articles to make study and recall easier
5. We have divided the Canons into 52 parts, to enable weekly

---

[1] The Latin version of the Westminster Confession was printed nine years after the English version.

reflection throughout the year.
6. Each of the main parts had positive and negative sections. Firstly an exposition of the Reformed doctrine is given on the subject. It is followed by a repudiation of corresponding Arminian errors. We have only reproduced the positive doctrinal statements here, as the rejections relate to specific positions taken by the Remonstrants at the time of the Synod. The rejections add little to the clear and full statements of Scripture truth made by this great Council.
7. Unlike many of the Reformation Confessions and Catechisms, the Canons of the Synod of Dort were not accompanied by an array of proof texts. In line with the object of this translation to encourage meditation and study, we have added suggested Scripture readings.
8. The Synod's Latin quotation of Scripture does not closely represent any known translation. At times it simply gives the sense of the reference. We have not 'corrected' it to any version.

We pray that this great Confession and these Scriptural truths will be better understood and valued by believers through the method of presentation that we have adopted.

We pray too that the glorious Gospel of God's electing and redeeming grace, presented in this booklet, may turn some from darkness to light, and from the power of Satan to God.

HOW TO USE THIS BOOK

There is great benefit in every line of this document. It should warm the heart of every believer.

We have set out the conclusions of the Synod on the page in a way that enables the reader to see the logic and connection of each statement made.

We suggest it be read slowly and thoughtfully, hovering over every line

We have divided the Articles into 52 portions, and suggest that they be used throughout the year, perhaps on a Sunday afternoon, for quiet thought, prayer, and praise

The accompanying Bible Reading can follow.

OPENING PRAYER

We ask each reader of this booklet to join in the prayer that concludes these Articles:

May the Son of God, Jesus Christ,

    Who,

        seated at the right hand of the Father,

            gives gifts to men

sanctify us in the truth

lead to the truth those who err

shut the mouths of those who make false accusations about sound doctrine

equip the faithful ministers of his Word with a spirit of wisdom and discretion

    that everything they eloquently speak

        may be to the glory of God

        and the edification of their hearers

                              Amen

Arrangement for weekly use

Week	Unconditional Election. Part 1	
1	God was under no obligation to save us	Article 1
2	How God's love is plainly shown How God enables men to believe the Gospel	Article 2 Article 3
3	The two responses to the Gospel and the two outcomes	Article 4
4	The cause of unbelief and the gift of faith	Article 5
5	Saving faith comes from God's eternal decree	Article 6
6	A definition of election	Article 7
7	The oneness of his elect people	Article 8
8	Faith, holiness, etc are the result of election, not the grounds for it	Article 9
9	God's sovereign kindness is the sole basis of election	Article 10
10	God's election is as unchangeable as he is The assurance and evidence of election	Article 11 Article 12
11	Assurance of election produces good fruit	Article 13
12	How and why the doctrine of election is to be made known	Article 14

13	God's rejection of unregenerate men explained (God's decree of reprobation)	Article 15
14	The right use of the doctrine of reprobation	Article 16
15	The security of children of the elect who die in infancy	Article 17
16	We cannot question God's decisions concerning election and reprobation	Article 18

Particular Redemption (Limited Atonement). Part 2

17	God's justice requires the full punishment of our sins	Article 1
18	The suretyship and satisfaction of Christ	Article 2
	The infinite value of Christ's sacrifice and satisfaction for sin	Article 3
19	Why Christ's death has such great value	Article 4
20	The promise of the Gospel should be freely proclaimed	Article 5
21	The failure of many to repent and be saved is not due to any defect in Christ's saving work	Article 6
	The salvation of sinners is by grace alone	Article 7
22	The full salvation of all those, and only those, whom God has chosen	Article 8
23	The Church of God will be gathered and kept through all ages	Article 9

Total Depravity and Irresistible Grace. Parts 3 and 4

24	Man's state before and after the Fall	Article 1

25	All the children of Adam are corrupt, except Christ alone	Article 2
	Man's present hopeless and helpless state	Article 3
26	The 'light of nature' cannot convert	Article 4
27	We cannot be saved by the Law	Article 5
28	How God saves	Article 6
29	The mystery of God's will and how we should respond	Article 7
30	God's genuine and sincere call to life and peace	Article 8
31	It is not any fault in the Gospel that men fail to come and be saved	Article 9
32	When the Gospel call is effectual it is wholly God's work	Article 10
33	What God does to a man's mind, heart, and will when he is saved	Article 11
34	The supernatural work of conversion that God works in us without us	Article 12
35	We cannot understand how God works in conversion	Article 13
	Both faith, and the will to believe, are the gift of God	Article 14
36	Attitudes that result from this doctrine	Article 15
37	How God works upon and renews man's will	Article 16
38	God's use of means in the regeneration of the elect	Article 17

The Perseverance of the Elect. Part 5

39	Regeneration does not wholly free us from our sinful nature	Article 1

40	How our sinful nature affects the life of a Christian	Article 2
	Christians cannot continue in grace in their own strength	Article 3
41	Christians sometimes backslide and commit grave sins	Article 4
42	The consequences of a Christian's backsliding and sin	Article 5
43	God never allows the elect to be finally lost	Article 6
44	God will restore his elect from their sins and backslidings	Article 7
45	Why the elect can never be lost	Article 8
46	The elect can, and do, have assurance of perseverance	Article 9
47	How the elect experience and know this assurance	Article 10
48	Carnal doubts and how God deals with them	Article 11
49	The fruits of assurance in the believer's life	Article 12
50	The effect of assurance of perseverance on restored backsliders	Article 13
51	How God continues and perfects the work of grace in us	Article 14
52	This doctrine is hated by the enemies of God, but loved by the Church	Article 15

FIRST POINT OF DOCTRINE

UNCONDITIONAL ELECTION

Part 1 Predestination (Unconditional Election)

Article 1. God was under no obligation to save us

Since

    all men have sinned in Adam

    lie under the curse

        and eternal death.

God would have done no one an injustice, if it had been his will

    to leave the whole human race in sin   and

        under the curse   and

to condemn it on account of sin.

According to the words of the Apostle

    All the world is liable to God's condemnation (Rom.3:19).

    All have sinned, and are destitute of the glory of God (Rom. 3:23).

    The wages of sin is death (Rom. 6:23).

<u>SUGGESTED READING: ROMANS 3</u>

Article 2. How God's love is plainly shown

Truly, in this the love of God is manifested
> that he sent his only begotten Son into the world
>> that whosoever believes in him
>>> should not perish
>>>> but have everlasting life.

In this was manifested the love of God toward us, because that God sent his only begotten Son into the world, that we might live through him (1 John 4:9).

For God so loved the world, that he gave his only begotten Son, that whosoever believes in him should not perish, but have everlasting life (John 3:16).

<u>SUGGESTED READING: JOHN 3</u>

Article 3. How God enables men to believe the Gospel

So that men may be brought to faith,

>God mercifully sends messengers of these most joyful tidings
>>to whom he will and
>>when he will
>by whose ministry men are called to repentance and faith in Christ crucified.

>*How shall they believe in him of whom they have not heard?*
>*How shall they hear without a preacher?*
>*How shall they preach, except they be sent?*
>>(Romans 10:14-15).

>>S<small>UGGESTED</small> R<small>EADING</small>: R<small>OMANS</small> 10

Article 4. The two responses to the Gospel and the two outcomes

Those who do not believe this Gospel
>> the wrath of God remains upon them.

But those who
>> receive it   and
>>>> embrace the Saviour Jesus by a true and living faith
>>>> are delivered by him
>>>>>> from the wrath of God   and
>>>>>> from destruction   and
>>>> receive the gift of eternal life.

<u>SUGGESTED READING: PSALM 1</u>

Part 1 Predestination (Unconditional Election)

Article 5. The cause of unbelief and the gift of faith

The cause, or guilt, of this unbelief
   as well as of all other sins
  is not at all in God
  but in man himself.

On the other hand
  faith in Jesus Christ, and
  salvation through him
    is the free gift of God.

As it is written:
  For by <u>grace</u> are ye saved through faith
   and that not of yourselves
   it is the gift of God (Eph. 2:8).

  Grace is given to you to believe in Christ (Phil. 1:29).

  <u>SUGGESTED READING: EPHESIANS 2:1-13</u>

Article 6. Saving faith comes from God's eternal decree

That (in time)
> some receive the faith that God gives   and
> others do not receive it
>> results from God's eternal <u>decree</u>.

Known unto God are all his works from the beginning of the world (Acts 15:18). *Who works all things after the counsel of his own will* (Eph. 1:11).

According to this <u>decree</u>
> the hearts of the elect, however hard
>> he graciously softens   and
>> inclines them to believe

While, in his just judgement
> he leaves the non-<u>elect</u>
>> to their own wickedness   and
>> hardness.

And in this is especially displayed to us the
> Profound, Merciful and (at the same time) Just
distinction between men equally ruined.

This is that <u>decree</u> of <u>election</u> and reprobation revealed in the Word of God, which
> though perverse, impure, and unstable men distort it to their own destruction
>> yet to holy and God-fearing souls
It provides <u>solace</u> that words cannot express.

<u>SUGGESTED READING: EPHESIANS 1:1-14</u>

Article 7. A definition of election

<u>Election</u> is the unchangeable purpose of God

By which,
> before the foundation of the world
> from the whole human race
>> (fallen by their own fault from their original integrity[1] into sin and destruction)
>
> according to the sovereign <u>good pleasure</u> of his own will
> purely by <u>grace</u>.

He has chosen to salvation in Christ
> a specific number of persons
>> (neither better nor more deserving than the others, but cast down with them in common misery)

[In Christ] whom he appointed from eternity to be
> The Mediator   and
> The Head of the all the <u>elect</u>   and
> The Foundation of salvation.

(Continued …)

Part 1 Predestination (Unconditional Election)

And thus <u>decreed</u>
    to give to Christ those who were to be saved by him   and
    to <u>effectually</u> call and draw them to his fellowship
        by his Word and Spirit
    to give them true faith
    to justify them   and
    to sanctify them   and
        having powerfully <u>watched over and kept</u> them in the fellowship of his Son
    to glorify them at last

for the demonstration of his mercy   and
for the praise of the riches of his glorious <u>grace</u>.   As it is written

'God chose us in Christ before the foundation of the world that we should be holy and without blame before him in love, having predestinated us to the adoption of children by Jesus Christ to himself according to the <u>good pleasure</u> of his will to the praise of the glory of his <u>grace</u>, in which he has made us accepted in the <u>Beloved</u>' (Eph. 1:4-6).

    And elsewhere:

'Whom he did predestinate, them he also called: and whom he called, them he also justified: and whom he justified them he also glorified' (Rom. 8:30).

SUGGESTED READING: REVELATION 5

Article 8. The oneness of his elect people

This <u>election</u> is not of different kinds
    but is one and the same for all those saved
        both under the Old and the New Covenant   for

Scripture declares the oneness of the will of God
    in his <u>good pleasure</u>, purpose, and <u>counsel</u>
        By which he has chosen us
            from eternity   both
            to <u>grace</u>   and
            to glory   both
            to salvation   and
            to the way of salvation,
                which he has prepared for us
                that we should walk in it

<u>SUGGESTED READING: GALATIANS 3</u>

Article 9. Faith, holiness, etc are the result of election not the grounds for it

This <u>election</u> was not based on
        foreseen faith
        the obedience of faith
        holiness   or
        any other good quality or disposition in man
    as the prerequisite cause or condition in the man to be chosen

But [men are chosen] to faith and the obedience of faith, holiness, and so on.

Therefore, <u>election</u> is the source of every saving benefit
    From it flows
        faith
        holiness   and
        the other gifts of salvation   and at last
        eternal life itself
    as its fruit and effect.

According to the Apostle:
He has chosen us (not because we were, but) *that we should be holy and without blame before him in love* (Eph. 1:4).[2]

<u>Suggested Reading: Ezekiel 16:1-14</u>

Article 10. God's sovereign kindness is the sole basis of election

The cause of this undeserved <u>election</u> is solely the <u>good pleasure</u> of God.

It does not consist in this -

> 'that, out of all possible qualities and actions of men, God has chosen some as a condition of salvation';

But

> 'that out of the common mass of sinners he took to himself certain specific persons as a personal possession'.

As it is written

> *For the children being not yet born, neither having done any good or evil.* (Rom. 9:11ff).
>
> *It was said (to Rebekah): 'The elder shall serve the younger'* (Gen. 25:23, Rom. 9:12).
>
> *As it is written, Jacob have I <u>loved</u>, but Esau have I hated* (Rom. 9:13).
>
> *Also 'As many as were ordained to eternal life believed'* (Acts 13:48).

<u>SUGGESTED READING: ROMANS 9:1-13</u>

Article 11. God's election is as unchangeable as God himself

As God himself is

> most wise
>
> unchangeable
>
> all-knowing and
>
> all-powerful

so, his <u>election</u> cannot be

> broken off
>
> altered
>
> revoked or
>
> annulled.

Neither can the <u>elect</u> be cast away

Nor their number be reduced.

<u>SUGGESTED READING: JAMES 1:1-18</u>

Part 1 Predestination (Unconditional Election)

Article 12. The assurance and evidence of election

Of this eternal and unchangeable <u>election</u> to their salvation

    His <u>elect</u> are made <u>certain</u>

        in due time   *though*

        by various stages   *and*

        in different measure

Not by inquisitively prying into the hidden and deep things of God

But by observing in themselves with spiritual joy and holy delight

    The unfailing fruit of election

        as indicated in the Word of God

    Namely, that they have:

        a true faith in Christ

        a childlike fear of God

        a godly sorrow for sin

        a hungering and thirsting after righteousness   *and so on*

<u>SUGGESTED READING: 1 JOHN 3</u>

Article 13. Assurance of election produces good fruit

Their <u>sense</u> and <u>certainty</u> of this <u>election</u>
> gives to the children of God greater cause
>> to daily
>>> humble themselves before God
>>> adore the fathomless depth of his mercies
>>> cleanse themselves and
>>> give fervent <u>love</u> in return
>>>> to him who first loved them so greatly.

This is far removed from saying that
> this doctrine of <u>election</u> and
> the consideration of it
>> makes them
>>> slow to keep the commands of God or
>>> unspiritual and <u>unconcerned</u>.

Rather
> in the just judgement of God
>> Those things usually occur
>>> in those who
>>>> Presume rashly or
>>>> Talk idly and boldly
>>>>> about the <u>grace</u> of <u>election</u>

> in those who refuse to walk in the ways of the <u>elect</u>.

<u>SUGGESTED READING: LUKE 7:36-50</u>

Part 1 Predestination (Unconditional Election)

Article 14. How and why the doctrine of election is to be made known

As the doctrine of Divine <u>election</u>
    according to the most wise <u>counsel</u> of God

was declared
    by the prophets
    by Christ himself and
    by the Apostles
    under both the Old and New Covenants and

was then committed to writing in the Holy Scriptures

So also today
    in the Church of God
        for which it was particularly intended

it is to be <u>proclaimed</u>
    with a spirit of discretion
    in a godly and holy manner
    in its place and time
    without delving curiously into the ways of the Most High

  for the glory of God's most holy name and
  for the strong[3] <u>solace</u> of his people.

<u>SUGGESTED READING: ROMANS 11</u>

Article 15. God's rejection of unregenerate men explained
(God's decree of reprobation)

This eternal and unmerited <u>grace</u> of our <u>election</u>
 is especially made clear and committed to us in writing
  in Holy Scripture
 when it testifies
  that not all men are <u>elect</u>
  but that some are non-<u>elect</u>
   passed by in the eternal <u>election</u> of God.

It is clear that God <u>decreed</u>
  out of his most free, most just, blameless, and unchangeable good pleasure
 to leave them in the common misery
  into which they
   by their own fault,
    have plunged themselves   and

 not to give them saving faith and the <u>grace</u> of conversion   but
  to leave them
   in their own ways   and
   under his just judgement   not only
    on account of their unbelief   but also
    for all their other sins

 for the clear manifestation of his justice
  to condemn   and
  to eternally punish them.

         (Continued …)

Part 1 Predestination (Unconditional Election)

This is the <u>decree</u> of reprobation
>which by no means makes God the Author of sin
>>(that is a blasphemous thought).

But rather

It establishes him as
>the fearsome, blameless, and just
>Judge and Avenger of sin.

<u>S</u>UGGESTED <u>R</u>EADING: <u>R</u>OMANS 9:14-24

Article 16. The right use of the doctrine of reprobation

Those who do not yet <u>effectually</u> <u>discern</u> in themselves

    a living faith in Christ
    an assured confidence of heart
    peace of conscience
    a zeal for childlike obedience   and
    a glorying in God through Christ

Yet who persist in the use of the means

    through which God has promised to work these graces in us

Ought not

    to be alarmed at the mention of reprobation
    to consider themselves among the reprobate

But should

    diligently persevere in the use of these means   and
    fervently desire   and
    reverently and humbly expect

        to receive a time of more abundant <u>grace</u>.

(Continued ...)

Part 1 Predestination (Unconditional Election)

Those who <u>seriously</u> desire
> to be turned to God
> to please him only and
> to be delivered from the body of death

> Yet who cannot reach that measure of holiness and faith
>> to which they aspire

>> have much less cause to be terrified by the doctrine of reprobation.

>>> Since the merciful God has promised
>>>> He will not quench the smoking flax and
>>>> He will not break the bruised reed (Isa. 42:3)

But this doctrine is deservedly a terror to those
> who have forgotten God and the Saviour Jesus Christ and
> who have wholly given themselves up
>> to the cares of the world and
>> to the sensual pleasures of the flesh

> for as long as they do not <u>seriously</u> turn to God.

<u>SUGGESTED READING: ISAIAH 42</u>

Article 17. The security of children of the elect who die in infancy[1]

Since we are to determine[2] the will of God from his Word
    which testifies that the children of believers are holy (1 Cor. 7:14)
        not by nature
        but as a benefit of the covenant of grace
            in which they
                together with the parents
            are included.

<u>Godly</u> parents ought not to doubt
        the <u>election</u> and salvation of their children
            whom God calls out of this life
                in infancy.

SUGGESTED READING: PSALM 103

---

[1] This article has particular reference to the false allegation of the Arminians, that, according to Reformed doctrine, 'Many children of believers are torn from their mothers' breasts and tyrannically thrown into Hell' (Conclusion, Canons of the Synod of Dort). This article presents covenant theology, which recognises the special position of the children of believers under the New, as well as in the Old Covenants (compare, for example, Acts 2:39 and Deuteronomy 30:6).
See also *Westminster Confession* 10.3.

[2] Determine: literally 'to judge', to come to conclusion about'.

Article 18. We cannot question God's decisions concerning election and reprobation

To those who complain against
> this <u>grace</u> of undeserved <u>election</u> and
> the severity of just reprobation

We set this of the Apostle in reply:
> *'O man, who are you who answers back against God?'* (Rom. 9:20).

So also our Saviour:
> *'Is it not lawful for me to do what I will with the things that are mine?'* *(Matthew 20:15).*

And therefore, with holy adoration of these mysteries
> We exclaim in the words of the Apostle:

'O the depth of the riches both of the wisdom and knowledge of God. How unsearchable are his judgements and his ways past finding out! For who has known the mind of the Lord? Or who has been his counsellor? Or who has first given to him, and it shall be paid back to him again?

> *For of him, and through him and to him are all things.*
> *To whom be glory for ever. Amen'* *(Romans 11:33-36).*

SUGGESTED READING: JOB 40-42:6

SECOND POINT OF DOCTRINE

Particular Redemption (or Limited Atonement)

Part 2 Limited Atonement (or Particular Redemption)

Article 1. God's justice requires the full punishment of our sins

God is   not only supremely merciful   but also
supremely just

His justice requires   (just as he himself has revealed in the Word)

that our sins   committed against his infinite majesty

should be surely punished[1]   not only with temporal

but with eternal punishment

both in soul and body

which punishment we cannot escape

unless satisfaction be made

to the justice of God.

SUGGESTED READING: REVELATION 20:11-15

---

[1] Literally 'punished with penalties'

Part 2 Limited Atonement (or Particular Redemption)

Article 2. The suretyship and satisfaction of Christ

Since we certainly cannot
    make <u>satisfaction</u> ourselves
    deliver ourselves from the wrath of God

God gave his only begotten Son
    out of his infinite mercy
as our Surety[4].

He was made
    sin and a curse on the cross
        to make <u>satisfaction</u>
            for us (or in our place).

SUGGESTED READING: ROMANS 5

Article 3. The infinite value of Christ's sacrifice and satisfaction for sin

The death of the Son of God is
    the only and most perfect
        sacrificial offering
    <u>satisfaction</u> for sin

of infinite worth and value
abundantly sufficient to expiate[5]
    the sins of the whole world.

SUGGESTED READING: HEBREWS 9:24-10:22

Part 2 Limited Atonement (or Particular Redemption)

Article 4. Why Christ's death has such great value

This death is of such great value and worth because

    the Person who was subject to it is   *not only*

        a true and perfectly holy man   *but also*

        the only begotten Son of God

            of the same eternal and infinite essence

                with the Father

                and the Holy Spirit

        as was necessary to be our Saviour   *and*

His death was joined with

    the <u>sense</u> of

        the wrath of God   *and*

        cursing

            which we

                by our sins

                    had fully deserved.

<u>SUGGESTED READING: HEBREWS 1-2:4</u>

Part 2 Limited Atonement (or Particular Redemption)

Article 5. The promise of the Gospel should be freely proclaimed

The promise of the Gospel is
>that whoever believes in Christ crucified
>>shall not be lost but
>>have everlasting life.

This promise
>ought to be declared and proclaimed
>>without differentiation or discrimination
>>>to all peoples and all men
>>>>to whom God out of his <u>good pleasure</u>
>>>>>sends the Gospel
>>>together with the command
>>>>to repent and believe.

<u>SUGGESTED READING: ACTS 17:16-34</u>

Part 2 Limited Atonement (or Particular Redemption)

Article 6. The failure of many to repent and be saved is not due to any defect in Christ's saving work

That many who are called by the Gospel
    do not repent
    do not believe in Christ   but
    are lost in unbelief

        is not from any defect or insufficiency
            in the sacrifice
                offered by Christ upon the cross   but

    It is from their own fault.

<u>SUGGESTED READING: MATTHEW 22:1-14</u>

Article 7. The salvation of sinners is by grace alone

But to as many as
    truly believe   and
        through the death of Christ
    are freed and saved
        from sins and ruin

    this benefit comes to them from the <u>grace</u> of God alone
        which he owes to no-one.
    It is given to them in Christ from eternity.

<u>SUGGESTED READING: TITUS 3</u>

Part 2 Limited Atonement (or Particular Redemption)

Article 8. The full salvation of all those, and only those, whom God has chosen

This was the sovereign <u>counsel</u>, and most gracious will and intention of God the Father
    that his Son's most precious death
        - life-giving and <u>efficacious</u> for salvation
    should extend to all the <u>elect</u>
        to give justifying faith to them alone,   and by it
        to bring them without fail to salvation.

This means:

God willed that Christ
    through the blood of the cross
        (by which he confirmed the new covenant)
    should <u>effectually</u> redeem
        out of every people, tribe, nation, and language
    all those   and
    those only
        who were from eternity
            elect to salvation   and
            given to him by the Father.

(Continued …)

Part 2 Limited Atonement (or Particular Redemption)

that he should
- give them faith
  (which together with the other saving gifts of the Holy Spirit, he acquired for them by his death)
- cleanse them by his blood from all sin
  - both original and actual
  - whether committed after faith or before faith
- <u>watch over and keep</u> them faithfully
  - all the way to the end
- present them glorious in his own presence at last
  - without any spot or blemish.

<u>Suggested Reading: Isaiah 53</u>

Part 2 Limited Atonement (or Particular Redemption)

Article 9. The Church of God will be gathered and kept through all ages

This <u>counsel</u>
    arising from love towards the <u>elect</u> from eternity
 has been powerfully accomplished
   from the beginning of the world
   to this present time   and
   will be from this time
     despite the useless attempts to frustrate it
      by the gates of hell.

Thus
 the elect will be gathered together into one
   in their time   and

 there will always be a Church of believers
   founded in the blood of Christ
    which steadfastly <u>loves</u> him   and
    which faithfully serves him
     as her Saviour
      (who, as a bridegroom for his bride
       laid down his life[6] for her
        upon the cross)
    which celebrates his praises
     here and through all eternity.

<u>Suggested Reading: Ephesians 5:22-33</u>

Part 2 Limited Atonement (or Particular Redemption)

THIRD AND FOURTH POINTS OF DOCTRINE

TOTAL DEPRAVITY AND IRRESISTIBLE GRACE

Article 1. Man's state before and after the Fall

Man was formed in the image of God from the beginning:
- his mind — was adorned with a true and wholesome knowledge of his Creator, and of spiritual things
- his will and heart — were upright
- his affections — were all pure.

So much so that he was completely holy

But — by rebelling against God
at the instigation of the devil
by his free own will
He has deprived himself of these excellent gifts.

He has brought on himself the opposite
in mind
- blindness
- terrible darkness
- vanity
- perverseness of judgement

in will and heart
- wickedness
- rebelliousness
- stubbornness

in all affections
- impurity.

SUGGESTED READING: GENESIS 2:7-3:24

Article 2. All the children of Adam are corrupt, except Christ alone

After the Fall
Man has brought forth children like himself.
    Corrupt, he produced corrupt [children].

Corruption has spread from Adam to all his posterity
    (with the exception of Christ alone)
    not by imitation   (as the Pelagians of old asserted)
    but by the propagation of a corrupt nature
according to God's just judgement.

<u>SUGGESTED READING: PSALM 51</u>

Article 3. Man's present hopeless and helpless state

Therefore, all men are
    conceived in sin   and
    children of wrath by nature
    incapable of any saving good
    inclined to evil
    dead in sin   and
    slaves to sin   and

Without the regenerating <u>grace</u> of the Holy Spirit
    they are neither able nor willing
        to return to God
        to reform the depravity of their nature   or even
        to make themselves ready for its reformation.

<u>SUGGESTED READING: EZEKIEL 37:1-14</u>

Article 4. The 'light of nature' cannot convert

There certainly remains some light of nature in man since the Fall
    by which
        he retains certain ideas about
            God
            natural things
            what is honourable and what is shameful   and
        he shows some regard for
            virtue and
            outward order.

But this light of nature is so far from
        reaching to a saving knowledge of God   and
        enabling true conversion
            that he is incapable of using it rightly
                even in natural and civil matters.

But yet further
        this light   (whatever it may be)
            he wholly pollutes in various ways   and
            he suppresses in unrighteousness.

                by so doing

He renders himself inexcusable before God.

<u>SUGGESTED READING: ROMANS 1:18-32</u>

Article 5. We cannot be saved by the Law

What applies to the light of nature likewise applies to
 the law of Ten Commandments
  which was
   through Moses
    especially[7] delivered
     by God
      to the Jews.

For though
 it shows the greatness of sin   and
 it convicts man more and more of his guilt

Yet
 it does not offer a remedy
 it does not grant strength to get out of distress.

Rather than that
   by the weakness of the flesh
 it leaves the transgressor under the curse.

Man cannot obtain saving grace by it.

SUGGESTED READING: ROMANS 7

Article 6. How God saves

What therefore neither the light of nature nor the law can do

    God performs

        by the power of the Holy Spirit

        through the word (or 'the ministry of reconciliation')

            which is the Gospel of the Messiah

                through which it has pleased God

                    to save those who believe

                        under both the Old,   and

                        under the New Covenant.

        SUGGESTED READING: 1 THESSALONIANS 1

Article 7. The mystery of God's will
and how we should respond

This mystery of God's will
    He revealed
        under the Old Covenant   - to few
        under the New Covenant   - to many
            (the distinction between the peoples
                having been removed)

The reason for this different arrangement is
    not the worthiness of one nation above another
    nor better use of the light of nature   but

It is the appointment of the sovereign <u>good pleasure</u>
    and undeserved love of God.

Hence,
    they to whom such <u>grace</u> is appointed
        beyond and contrary to all they deserve
    ought to acknowledge it
        with a humble and thankful heart.

But in regard to the others
    to whom this <u>grace</u> is not given
        they ought to adore
            the severity and justice of God's judgements
        with the Apostle
    (we should certainly not inquisitively pry into them).

<u>SUGGESTED READING: EPHESIANS 3</u>

Article 8. God's genuine and sincere call to life and peace

As many as are called by the Gospel are <u>seriously</u> called

    For God
        <u>seriously</u> and
        most sincerely
    makes known
        in his Word
    what is pleasing to him.
So that those who are called should come to him.

He also <u>seriously</u> promises
    to all who
        come to him and
        believe
rest to their souls and
eternal life.

<u>SUGGESTED READING: ISAIAH 55</u>

Article 9. It is not any fault in the Gospel that men fail to come and be saved

That many
    who are called through the ministry of the Gospel
do not come   and
are not converted

is not a fault
    in the Gospel   nor
    in Christ   offered in the Gospel   nor
    in God   who calls through the Gospel   and even
        <u>grants</u> them various gifts.

But the fault lies in the persons themselves who are called

    Some who are <u>unconcerned</u>
        do not <u>receive to themselves</u> the word of life

    Others <u>receive it to themselves</u>
        <u>but do not receive it into their heart</u>   and therefore
        after the fading joy of a temporary faith
        they turn back.

    Others choke the seed of the Word
        by the thorns of the cares and sensual pleasures
            of this age
    and produce no fruit.

This our Saviour teaches in the Parable of the Sower (Matt. 13).

<u>SUGGESTED READING: MATTHEW 13:1-23</u>

Article 10. When the Gospel call is effectual it is wholly God's work

When others
>who are called through the ministry of the Gospel

do come and are converted

It is not to be attributed to man
>as if by free <u>choice</u> they distinguish themselves from others
>>who have equal or sufficient <u>grace</u>
>>>for faith and conversion
>>>>(as the proud heresy of Pelagius maintains).

But it must be attributed to God
>who from eternity chose his own in Christ.

So that, in time
>he <u>effectually</u> calls them
>he gives them faith and repentance
>>and, having rescued them from the power of darkness
>he transfers them into the kingdom of his Son.

So that they may declare the wonderful deeds of him
>who brought them out of darkness into his marvellous light

That they may not glory in themselves, but in the Lord.

As the writing of the Apostles[1] testifies in various places.

<u>SUGGESTED READING: JOHN 10</u>

---

[1] Literally 'apostolic writing' or 'apostolic Scripture'. It is therefore not clear whether this is a reference to the Apostle Paul only or not.

Article 11. What God does to a man's mind, heart, and will when he is saved

When God carries out his <u>good pleasure</u> in the <u>elect</u>
    (or works in them true conversion)
He not only
    takes care that the Gospel is outwardly preached to them   and
    powerfully enlightens their mind by his Holy Spirit
        that they may rightly understand and distinguish
            the things of the Spirit of God.
But also
    by the <u>effectual</u> working of the same regenerating Spirit
        penetrates to the innermost parts of the man
        opens the closed heart   and
        softens the hardened heart
        circumcises that which was uncircumcised
        infuses new qualities into the will   and
        makes the will

from being dead	alive
from being bad	good
from being unwilling	willing
from being stubborn	compliant

        He moves it and strengthens it
            so that
                like a good tree
                    it may produce the fruit of good works.

<u>SUGGESTED READING: COLOSSIANS 1</u>

Article 12. The supernatural work of conversion that God works in us without us

And this is what is so much proclaimed in the Scriptures:
> the regeneration
> the new creation
> the resurrection from the dead
> the making alive

which God works in us without us.

But this is certainly not brought about merely
> by outward teaching
> by moral persuasion
> or such a way of working
>> that, after God had done his work
>>> it still remains in man's power
>>>> to be regenerated or unregenerate
>>>> to be converted or unconverted.

But it is evidently a work that is
> supernatural
> most powerful   and at the same time
> most delightful
> wonderful
> mysterious   and
> inexpressible.

(Continued ...)

Part 3 and 4 Total Depravity and Irresistible Grace

Its power, according to Scripture
    (which is inspired by the Author of this working)
is not less than, or inferior to,
    creation,   or
        the resurrection from the dead.

So that
    all those in whose hearts God works in this amazing way are
        <u>certainly</u>
        infallibly   and
        <u>efficaciously</u>
    regenerated   and
    do in fact believe.

Indeed,
    the will
        then renewed
            is not only acted upon and moved by God
                but having been acted upon
                    it also acts.

Therefore, a man himself is rightly said
    to believe and repent
        through the <u>grace</u> he has received.

<u>SUGGESTED READING: JOHN 11:1-44</u>

Article 13. We cannot understand how God works in conversion

The way this works cannot be fully comprehended by believers in this life.

   In the meantime,

      they rest quietly

         they know and

         they <u>discern</u>

            that by this <u>grace</u> of God

               they believe with the heart

               and <u>love</u> their Saviour.

<u>Suggested Reading: Psalm 90</u>

Article 14. Both faith, and the will to believe, are the gift of God

In this way therefore,
    Faith is the gift of God
    Not that it is offered by God for a man to <u>choose</u>
    But that it is actually
        <u>granted</u>
            breathed into   and
            infused

    Not even that God <u>grants</u> just the power to believe
        but then awaits
            consent   or
            the act of believing
                from man's <u>choice</u>

But because he <u>effects</u> in man both the will to believe and believing itself.

He works both willing and doing   and

Thus, he works all in all.[8]

<u>Suggested Reading: Acts 13:44-52</u>

Article 15. Attitudes that result from this doctrine

God owes this <u>grace</u> to no one.
> For what truly could he owe to one who is able to give nothing?
> How can he be repaid?
> What could he owe
>> to one who has nothing of his own but sin and falsehood?

Therefore,
> he who receives this <u>grace</u>
>> owes and gives eternal thanks
>>> solely to God.

Whoever does not receive it   either
> does not care at all about these spiritual things   and
> is self-satisfied   or else
> he has [false] security
>> and foolishly boasts that he has what he does not have.

(Continued ...)

Part 3 and 4 Total Depravity and Irresistible Grace

Regarding those who outwardly profess their faith and amend their lives
- we are to judge and speak the best of them
   - (according to the example of the Apostles)
- for the inmost parts of their heart are unknown to us.

As to others who have not yet been called
- We are to pray to God
   - who calls the things that are not, just as if they were[9].   but
- We are in no way to pride ourselves that we are better than them
   - as if we ourselves are in any way different[10].

<u>Suggested Reading: Psalm 116</u>

Part 3 and 4 Total Depravity and Irresistible Grace

Article 16. How God works upon and renews man's will

By the Fall,
    Man did not cease to be man,
        endowed with intellect and will
    Neither did sin
        (which has pervaded the whole human race)
    take away man's human nature
    But depraved it   and
        brought spiritual death.

So, neither does
This God-given <u>grace</u> of regeneration
        act upon men as trunks of wood and stumps   nor
        take away the will and its properties   nor
        force it with violence

    But   enlivens spiritually
        heals
        corrects   and at the same time
        sweetly and powerfully bends it[1].

(Continued ...)

---

[1] i.e., the will

So that
> where rebellion and resistance of the flesh were formerly completely dominant
>> now a ready and sincere obedience of the Spirit begins to reign
>>> in which the true and spiritual renewal and freedom of our will consists.

For this reason
> unless the wonderful Author of every good thing drives us to action
>> man could have no hope
>>> of recovering from the Fall
>>>> by his own free <u>choice</u>
>>>>> for by that
>>>>>> while he was yet standing
>>>>>>> he cast himself headlong into ruin.

S<small>UGGESTED</small> R<small>EADING</small>: A<small>CTS</small> 9:1-22

Article 17. God's use of means in the regeneration of the elect

Just as the almighty working of God
> by which he produces and sustains this our natural life

does not exclude, but requires, the use of means
> by which God
>> according to his infinite wisdom and goodness
>
> has willed to exercise this his power.

So also, the supernatural working of God
> spoken of already
>
> by which he regenerates us

in no way excludes, or overthrows, the use of the Gospel
> which the most wise God has ordained to be
>> the seed of regeneration and the food of the soul.

For this reason, the Apostles, and the teachers who succeeded them
> With <u>godly diligence</u> taught the people about this <u>grace</u> of God
>> to his glory and to the putting down of all pride.

(Continued …)

Part 3 and 4 Total Depravity and Irresistible Grace

But, at the same time
    they did not neglect to keep them
        by the holy Gospel warnings
    under the exercise of
        the Word
        the sacraments   and
        discipline.

So, even now, it is unthinkable[11]
    that either the teachers, or those taught, in the Church
        should dare to tempt God
            by separating those things
                which he in his <u>good pleasure</u> has willed
                    to be most closely joined together.

For <u>grace</u> is <u>granted</u> by warnings   and
    the more we readily perform what is required of us
        the clearer is this favour of God working in us
        and his work proceeds best.

        To him alone
   all the glory is due for ever
       for the means
  and for their saving fruit
     and <u>efficacy</u>
       Amen.

<u>SUGGESTED READING</u>: Acts 1:22-47

Part 3 and 4 Total Depravity and Irresistible Grace

FIFTH POINT OF DOCTRINE

THE PERSEVERANCE OF THE ELECT

(The Perseverance of the Saints)

Article 1. Regeneration does not wholly free us from our sinful nature

Those
> whom God
>> according to his purpose
>
> calls to the fellowship of his Son
>> our Lord Jesus Christ   and
>
> regenerates by the Holy Spirit

> he certainly sets free from
>> the dominion and slavery of sin
>
> although not entirely from
>> the flesh   and
>> the body of sin (Rom. 6:6)[12]
>>> in this life.

SUGGESTED READING: ROMANS 6

Part 5 The Perseverance of the Elect

Article 2. How our sinful nature affects the life of a Christian

As a result of this[1]

    Daily sins of weakness spring up   *and therefore*
    Blemishes cling even to the best works of the saints
        for which they continually have cause
            to be humble before God   *and*
            to flee for refuge to Christ crucified
            to put the flesh to death more and more
                by the spirit of supplications   *and*
                by holy and <u>godly diligence</u>   *and*
            to long after the goal of perfection
    until at last
        delivered from the body of death
            they reign with the Lamb of God in heaven.

<u>SUGGESTED READING: PSALM 32</u>

---

[1] Because of the incomplete deliverance from the flesh and the body of sin - i.e., Part 5 Article 1

Article 3. Christians cannot continue in grace in their own strength

Because of these
- remnants of indwelling sin
- the world
- the temptations of Satan

together with

those who have been converted could not remain standing in this <u>grace</u>
if left to their own strength.

But God is faithful
Who
once <u>grace</u> is bestowed on them
mercifully strengthens and
powerfully keeps them in it
to the end.

<u>Suggested Reading: Galatians 5:16-26</u>

Article 4. Christians sometimes backslide and commit grave sins

Although the power of God which confirms and preserves true believers in <u>grace</u> is so great that the flesh cannot overcome it.

Yet those who are converted are not always so moved and motivated by God
    that it should not be possible
        in certain particular actions
      to turn back from the leading of <u>grace</u>[13]
        through their own fault
      to be seduced by   and
      to indulge
        the lusts of the flesh.

They must therefore be constantly in watching and prayer
    that they may not be led into temptations.

When they fail to do this
    they not only *can be* dragged away by
        the flesh
        the world   and
        Satan
            into burdensome and terrible sins
but they *are* sometimes actually dragged away
    with God's just permission.

The sad falls of David, Peter, and other saints
    described in Holy Scripture
  demonstrate this.

<u>SUGGESTED READING: MATTHEW 26:57-75</u>

Article 5. The consequences of a Christian's backsliding and sin

But by such gross sins
they
    greatly offend God
    bring on themselves a deadly guilt
    grieve the Holy Spirit
    interrupt the exercise of faith
    very grievously wound their conscience
        and sometimes for a period
    lose the experience of [God's] grace

until
    by earnest repentance
    returning to the way of life

God's fatherly face again shines upon them.

SUGGESTED READING: 1 SAMUEL 11-12:23

Article 6. God never allows the elect to be finally lost

Truly, God
    who is rich in mercy,
        according to his unchangeable purpose of <u>election</u>
            even in their sad backslidings
does not wholly withdraw the Holy Spirit from his own   and
does not allow them to sink
    to fall away from
        the <u>grace</u> of adoption   and
        the state of justification   or
    to commit the sin unto death (the sin against the Holy Spirit)
        to be wholly deserted by him
        to cast themselves headlong into eternal ruin.

<u>Suggested Reading: Lamentations 3:1-41</u>

Article 7. God will restore his elect from their sins and backslidings

For, in the first place
> in these backslidings
>> he preserves his immortal seed[14] in them
>>> by which they are born again
>>> so that it is not lost and is not cast off.

Next
> by his Word and Spirit
> he <u>certainly</u> and <u>efficaciously</u> renews them to repentance[15]

So that
> they have heartfelt godly sorrow
>> on account of the sins that they have committed
>
> by faith
>> with a contrite heart
>>> they strive after, and obtain
>>>> forgiveness in the blood of the Mediator.

They then again
> <u>experience</u> the <u>grace</u> of a reconciled God
> adore his mercies by faith

and from then on
> they more diligently
> work out their own salvation with fear and trembling.

<u>SUGGESTED READING: JOHN 21:1-19</u>

Part 5 The Perseverance of the Elect

Article 8. Why the elect can never be lost

So, it is
    not by their own merits or strength
    but of God's free mercy
        that they obtain it
        that they do not
            totally fall away from faith and <u>grace</u> nor
            ultimately remain in their backslidings
                so that they should be lost.

    which (with respect to themselves)
        could not only easily happen
        but undoubtedly would happen.

    but (with respect to God)
        this cannot possibly happen.
since
        His <u>counsel</u> cannot be changed
        nor his promise fail,
        neither can the call according to his purpose be revoked
        nor the merit, intercession and <u>watchful keeping</u> of Christ
            be rendered ineffectual
        nor the sealing of the Holy Spirit[16] fail, or be removed.

<u>SUGGESTED READING: JOHN 17</u>

Article 9. The elect can and do have assurance of perseverance

Therefore

 of this <u>watchful keeping</u> of the <u>elect</u> to salvation   and
 of the <u>watchful keeping</u> in the faith of true believers

believers can, and do, have <u>certainty</u> in themselves
 according to the measure of their faith
  by which they <u>certainly</u> believe that
   they are and always will
    be true and living members of the church
   have forgiveness of sins
    and eternal life.

<u>SUGGESTED READING: HEBREWS 11</u>

Article 10. How the elect experience and know this assurance

Therefore
>This <u>certainty</u> is
>>Not from some special revelation
>>>beyond or extra to the Word
>>but from faith in the promises of God
>>>which he has most abundantly revealed in his Word
>>>>for our <u>solace</u>
>>from the testimony of
>>>*the Holy Spirit witnessing with our spirit that we are sons and heirs of God*
>>>>>>(Rom. 8:16)

>>from a <u>serious</u> and holy pursuit
>>>of a good conscience   and
>>>of good works.

>If in this world the <u>elect</u> of God were deprived
>>of this well-founded <u>solace</u> of obtaining the victory   and
>>of this unfailing guarantee of eternal glory

>They would be of all men the most miserable.

S<small>UGGESTED</small> R<small>EADING</small>: P<small>SALMS</small> 42 & 43

Article 11. Carnal doubts and how God deals with them

Nevertheless

    Scripture testifies that

        believers are assaulted in this life with various carnal doubts   and

            (placed under severe temptation)

        they do not always <u>sense</u>

            this full assurance of faith[17]   and

        <u>certainty</u> of perseverance.

But God

        Who is the Father of all consolation

            Does not let them be tempted above that they are able,

            but will with the temptation, also make a way to escape.

                                          (1 Corinthians 10:13)

    And, by the Holy Spirit

        He again awakens in them

            the <u>certainty</u> of perseverance.

<u>SUGGESTED READING: 1 CORINTHIANS 10:1-13</u>

Article 12. The fruits of assurance in the believer's life

This <u>certainty</u> of perseverance
   is so far from
      making believers proud   or
      making them unspiritual and <u>unconcerned</u>

   that on the contrary
      it is the true root of
         humility
         childlike reverence
         true <u>godliness</u>
         patience in every conflict[18]
         fervent prayers
         steadfastness
            in trouble[19]   and
            in confessing the truth   and
         lasting inward rejoicing in God.

   so that the consideration of this benefit is a stimulus
      to the serious and constant practice
         of gratitude and good works

   as is evident from
      the testimonies of Scripture   and
      the examples of the saints.

<u>Suggested Reading: Romans 8</u>

Article 13. The effect assurance of perseverance has on restored backsliders

Neither does renewed confidence of being <u>watched over and kept</u>
>> produce immorality or
>> neglect of <u>godliness</u>
>>> in those who have been restored from backsliding.

But it gives a much greater concern
> to carefully keep to the ways of the Lord
>> which are prepared in advance[20]
> that by walking in them
>> they may maintain the <u>certainty</u> of their perseverance.

Lest by the abuse of his fatherly goodness
> the face of their merciful God should turn away from them again
>> which to behold is sweeter than life
>> its withdrawal more bitter than death
with the result that they fall into greater agonies of the soul.

<u>Suggested Reading: 2 Corinthians 7</u>

Article 14. How God continues and perfects the work of grace in us

Just as it pleased God to begin this his work of <u>grace</u> in us
>by the preaching of the Gospel

So also
>by its
>>hearing
>>reading
>>thoughtful consideration
>>exhortations
>>threatenings
>>promises
>
>as well as by the use of the sacraments

He maintains, continues, and perfects it.

<u>SUGGESTED READING: PSALM 119:33-56</u>

Article 15. This doctrine is hated by the enemies of God but loved by the Church

This teaching regarding
    the perseverance of true believers and of the saints   and
    the <u>certainty</u> of it
        which God
            to the glory of his name   and
            the <u>solace</u> of <u>godly</u> souls
        has most abundantly revealed in his Word   and
    impresses on the hearts of the faithful
        the flesh does not understand
        Satan hates
        the world ridicules
        the ignorant and hypocrites abuse   and
        the heretics[1] attack

(Continued ...)

---

[1] Heretics. Literally 'spirits of error'

Part 5 The Perseverance of the Elect

But the Bride of Christ
> has always <u>loved</u> this teaching most tenderly
>> as a treasure of inestimable value   and
> has steadfastly defended it.

And God
> against whom
>> no counsel can have any effect   and
>> no strength can prevail

will ensure that it continues to do so

> **Now, to this God alone**
> **Father, Son, and Holy Spirit**
> **be honour and glory forever**
> **Amen.**

<u>Suggested Reading: Jude 1-25</u>

GLOSSARY

Certain, certainty, certainly: Latin, *certus* and its derivatives. These Latin words occur repeatedly in the Canons of Dort, particularly in relation to Part 5, the Perseverance of the saints. We have translated 'certain', 'certainty', 'certainly' throughout, but the Latin has a wider meaning of something decided, fixed, settled, or assured.

Choice, choose: Latin *arbitrio* to choose, *arbitrium* a choice or decision. Compare the English 'arbiter', one who makes a decision. This is used in the Canons of Dort in connection with man choosing. The Latin *liberum arbitrium* is usually translated 'free will', but the Latin word for 'will' (*voluntas*) is not present: we have translated 'free choice' for consistency. *Arbitrium* is not the word used in connection with God's 'choosing' or 'election' (q.v.).

Counsel: Latin *consilium*. In the Canons of Dort this almost always refers to 'the counsel of the will of God'. This is not God's 'decision' – as though 'he made a choice based on options' in a human sense. It is his eternal and unchangeable will. It refers in Part 2 Articles 8 and 9 to the 'counsel of peace' between God the Father and God the Son for the redemption of the elect.

Decree: Latin, *decretum, decerno* – 'The decree of God is his eternal plan or purpose, in which he has foreordained all things that come to pass' (Berkhof). By it, from eternity, God wills and orders all things. It is not conditional upon anything other than the will of God himself. See Muller, *Dictionary of Latin and Greek Theological Terms*.

Discern – see 'sense'

Dispensation: Latin *dispensatio*. This is the equivalent of the Greek word *oikonomia* (οικονομια). In Parts 3/4 Article 7 it relates to God's differing arrangements (administration) for man's redemption that have been evident at different times since man's Fall. It should be noted that this does not in any way indicate 'dispensationalism', which teaches that the nature of the Gospel has changed, and the preaching of Jesus differs from the preaching of Paul.

Effects: Latin *efficio, effectus*. We have translated these two words as 'effect' and as 'to effect', i.e., 'to bring about a result, to accomplish' – rather than simply 'works' in Article 3/4 Part 14. See also efficacious.

Efficacious, efficacy, and effectual: Latin *efficaciter, efficacia, efficax.* English (from the Latin) has various words that relate to producing an effect, although today the meaning is often blurred. Effective = 'powerful in effect'; Effectual applies to the action not the doer = 'achieving the complete effect aimed at'; Efficacious applies to things which 'produce (or are certain to produce) the desired effect'. See Fowler *A Dictionary of Modern English Usage*. We thus speak of an effectual call, but efficacious grace. The Synod of Dort affirms that, when God calls a man, it always has the effect that God desires, e.g., Part 1 Article 7, Part 5 Article 7. God never calls in vain. God's work is not just 'effective'. We have therefore sought to translate these Latin words precisely.

Elect, election: Latin *electio, electos, eligo*. The Synod of Dort defined the meaning of God's 'election' in Part 1 Article 7. Believers were chosen before the foundation of the world in Christ (Eph. 1:4) to be with him eternally. This was not on the basis of merit (Deut. 7:7, 8). This is the 'positive' part of predestination. The negative is 'reprobation', whereby the remainder (the 'non-elect') were justly left to bear the consequences of their sin. Reprobation is also a decree of God (Part 1 Article 15).

Experience: see 'sense'

Godly, godliness, godly diligence: Latin *pius, pietas*. This relates to faithfully doing with, reverential fear, what pleases God. It is the practical expression of love to God and man. *Pietas* is the frequent translation of the Greek word ευσεβεια *eusebeia* (AV 'godliness') in 1 Timothy and 2 Peter in the Vulgate and in Beza's Latin translation. The A.V. usually translates it 'godliness'. See the *New Bible Dictionary*, 'piety'.

Good pleasure: Latin *beneplacitum*. In Reformed theology this is only applied to God, as in Eph. 1:5 'the good pleasure' of his will. It is what is agreeable and right to God. It is hard to find a better translation than 'good pleasure' for this word or for the Greek equivalent (ευδοκια - *eudokia*). It is the appointment of the free purpose and undeserved love of God. It literally means 'that which is good and very pleasing', and is often linked with the word for 'will'. See Part 1 Article 15.

Grace: Latin *gratia*. Here, and throughout these Articles, this is 'the free and undeserved love or favour of God exercised toward the undeserving, toward sinners', Loraine Boetner, *The Reformed Doctrine of Predestination*.

Grant: Latin *confero*. All translations use 'conferred'. We have avoided this 'latinism' as it implies a transfer or imparting of grace, etc as though through some instrumentality, e.g., Parts 3/4 Article 17, which we might otherwise translate 'For grace is conferred by admonitions'.

Love: Where underlined this is the Latin verb *diligo*, 'to lovingly prize with diligence'. It is used of God's love to the elect - 'Jacob have I loved' (Part 1

Article 10) - as well as our love for Christ (Part 3/4 Article 13), and our love for the Word (Part 5 Article 15).

Receive it to themselves, but do not receive it into their heart: [Part 3/4 Article 9] 'to come to', or 'to receive to' Latin: *ad-mitto*. 'To enter' or 'to receive into': Latin: *im-mitto*. A distinction is made between the word being received and the word entering into them. The distinction is likewise in the Greek words for 'receive' in Mark 4:16 and 20. The point is that it is only when the word enters in and takes root in the heart that there is a true conversion. The standard translation 'allow to enter', etc is clearly unfortunate, as it implies the man has the free will to accept or not accept the word, which is explicitly rejected in Part 3/4 Article 14.

Satisfaction: Latin, *satisfactio, satisfacio.* to make reparation for, pay off, make amends for; as Christ met all the demands of Divine justice.

Sense, discern, experience: Latin *sensus*, and the verb *sentio* do not simply refer to something physical, known through the five senses. The meaning of the Latin word is given by Cassell's *Latin Dictionary* as three-fold – 1. Physical sensation, or feeling through the senses; 2. Emotional feeling, or sentiment, as experiencing love or joy; 3. Intellectual discerning, perceiving, understanding. It may be that all three are combined when, for example Part 2 Article 4 speaks of Christ's death being joined with the sense (*sensus*) of the wrath of God (see Luke 22:42, 44 and Matthew 27:46). It is closer there to the meaning of 'experiencing'. The word conveys more than a mere feeling, or a mental deduction, as is clear when the Canons speak of the 'sense' of certainty of conversion or preservation.

Serious, seriously: Latin *serio*, earnestly, unfeignedly. The meaning of the word is well illustrated in Part 3/4 Article 8, in which it is used three times. The offer of peace and life in the Gospel is honest, genuine, and serious. It is not a charade or pretence, as falsely alleged by the Arminians in arguing against God's purposes in election.

Solace: Latin *solatium* from *solatio*. We have used the Latin derived translation 'solace' rather than 'comfort', 'peace' or even 'consolation' (*consolatio* occurs in Part 5 Article 11). From its root meaning *solatio* conveys the idea of relief from distress, disappointment, or sorrow. In Christ we have such a solace.

The law of the Ten Commandments: Latin *haec Decalogi* Parts 3/4 Article 5. The Ten Commandments as a collective body of law; the clear, perfect, and complete rule of human conduct, only fulfilled in Christ.

Unconcerned: Latin *securus*, without anxiety or care. Part 3/4 Article 9. The English word 'security' has developed from it and the wider original meaning has been lost.

In Part 1 Article 13 and Part 5 Article 12 the Latin expression is *carnaliter securi*, 'carnally secure' – unconcerned because they live only for this outward physical life in the flesh; as Rom. 8:1-13. We have translated this expression 'unspiritual and unconcerned'.

Watched over and kept: Latin *custodia*, *custodio*, from *custos* a watchman or guardian. The believer is thus 'preserved' to his final blessedness in glory not in an abstract passive way, but by being actively kept by God.

FURTHER READING

We recommend the following:

Philip Schaff, *The Creeds of Christendom*, Volume 3. This gives the full text of the Canons of the Synod of Dort in Latin, with an English translation. Schaff's Latin text was used in this translation.

Peter G. Feenstra, *Unspeakable Comfort: A Commentary on The Canons of Dort*, Premier Publishing. This is a spiritual and doctrinal commentary, which draws out the answers to the Arminian error.

David Blunt, Jan Freeke, Joel R. Beeke, *The Synod of Dort and the Dutch Further Reformation*, The Presbyterian Standard, Issue 61. This is a brief and helpful all-round introduction to the Synod of Dort that summarises its key statements.

Joel R. Beeke, Sinclair Ferguson, *Reformed Confessions Harmonized*, Baker Books. This helpfully sets 'the three forms of unity' (The Belgic Confession, The Heidelberg Catechism, and the Canons of Dort) alongside the Westminster standards in a thematic arrangement. Unfortunately, it does not provide a way of unscrambling the arrangement to compare the Articles of the Synod with other Reformed statements consecutively. We had to prepare one ourselves!

Robert L. Dabney, Jonathan Dickinson, *The Five Points of Calvinism*, Sprinkle Publications. This combination of earlier books provides a helpful and clear statement of the doctrines defended at Dort, whilst not directly commenting on the Synod or the Canons as such.

ENDNOTES

[1] Integrity: Latin *integritate*. Man's original wholeness and purity in body, mind, and spirit, created in the image of God.

[2] i.e., not because we are, but so that we should be. See also Eph.1:5 and 2:10.

[3] Strong: here Latin *vividus*, literally 'lively', 'enlivening' – hence vigorous, strong.

[4] Surety: Latin *Sponsor*. A surety is 'A person who undertakes responsibility for another's performance of an undertaking, as the payment of a debt, appearance in court, etc' (SOED). The term is the equivalent of the Hebrew גאל – *goel* – kinsman-redeemer (Lev. 25:25, Psalm 19:14). Christ undertook, as man, to render to God whatever was due to God from man. In Part 2 Article 9 and Part 5 Article 15 the relation of the Church to Christ is called that of a Bridegroom to a Bride, with related words, *sponsus* and *sponsa*.

[5] Expiate. Latin *expio*. However, here the statement suggests 1 John 2:2 where Christ is described as the 'propitiation' for sins. To expiate means to remove or cleanse sin. To propitiate means to appease or turn aside a person's anger and make them favourable. 'God, at the very time when He loved us, was hostile to us until reconciled in Christ' Calvin, Institutes 2:17.2, Part 2 end of 3.

[6] Laid down his life: Latin *animam suam in cruce exposuit*. Literally 'exposed his soul on the cross'. The sufferings of Christ on the cross were both body and soul. See Berkhof *Systematic Theology* p. 337.

[7] Especially: Latin *peculiariter* – a word used of the Jews in Deuteronomy 7:6; 14:2; 26:18 – compare Romans 9:4.

[8] Works all in all. See Ephesians 1:23 and 1 Corinthians 12:6.

[9] Romans 4:17.

[10] Acts 15:9.

[11] Unthinkable: Latin, absit. Part 3-4 Art. 17. The Vulgate and Beza use this Latin word in Romans 3:6, etc, where the A.V. translates 'God forbid'.

[12] The body of sin. See Romans 6:6. Our sinful carnal nature, 'sin as it dwells in us in our present embodied state', Jamieson, Fausett and Brown, *Bible Commentary*.

[13] The leading of grace. Compare Hebrews 13:9. Perhaps meaning 'God's gracious leading'.

[14] 1 John 3:9; 1 Peter 1:23.

[15] Repentance. Latin *paenitentia*, contrition, regret. A different word to the one translated 'repentance' elsewhere in the Canons, e.g., Part 2 Article 5 and Part 5 Article 5 (*resipscentia*), where the meaning is closer to 'recovery' and 'restoration', as in 2 Timothy 2:26.

[16] 2 Corinthians 1:2.

[17] Full assurance, Latin *plerophoria* from the Greek πληροφορια, the word used in Heb.6:11 and 1 Thess. 1:5.

[18] Conflict. There are two possible meanings to the Latin word *lucta* here (Part 5 Article 12). Either it is a wrestling match, hence 'conflict', or it is the perfect passive participle of *lugeo*, to be in mourning, and therefore means here 'in every tribulation'.

[19] Steadfastness in trouble: Literally 'constancy in the cross'. Whilst the reference may be to affliction, it may also refer to the Saviour's word that we should take up our cross daily (Luke 9:23).

[20] Ephesians 2:10 – AV 'foreordained'.

Advertisement:

UPCOMING BOOKS BY PEARL PUBLICATIONS

It is intended (D.V.) to publish the following books in autumn – winter 2022-23.

1. A Help for using the Psalms in Personal and Family Worship
[hardback, paperback and E-book 440 pages]

2. Simply Psalms for Singing:
A translation for singing arranged in daily portions
[hardback, paperback and E-book 240 pages]

3. Simply Psalms for Singing: An Expanded Edition
[hardback, paperback and Ebook 380 pages]

The Psalms were the songbook of the Church from its very beginning. There is no evidence that the early Church had hymnbooks. In parts of the world the Biblical Psalms are still widely used. Elsewhere they have been largely displaced by worship songs and hymns. The 'Psalms' of hymn books usually bear little resemblance to the Psalms of the Bible.

Was the Church wrong to sing the Psalms almost exclusively for nearly 2,000 years, or have the modern Christians lost something that the Holy Spirit gave them to use? God gave the Psalms to be sung, and the New Testament urges us to sing them – but how?

These books on the Psalms go back to basics, and challenge Christians to sing

Advertisement:

the Psalms in their personal worship, and with their families. A scheme is provided to sing the Psalms through in a year. Short devotional and Bible study notes are provided for each day, with other materials to encourage thought and discussion. The *Help* discusses resources that can be used to sing the Psalms. One of these resources is its sister book, *Simply Psalms for Singing*.

Simply Psalms for Singing follows the same daily scheme, and translates the Psalms closely to the original Hebrew. It uses a single metre that enables anyone with knowledge of one or two familiar tunes (e.g. 'Abide with me') to sing through all the Psalms. The expanded edition of *Simply Psalms for Singing* goes to greater depth and is a valuable Bible study aid in working through the Psalms.

We believe that a great opportunity was missed by Churches, families and individuals during the time of Covid restrictions and lockdowns. Instead of online experimentation in worship, when 'logging in' replaced Church attendance, we believe personal and family worship should have been re-introduced widely. Family worship is now a rarity in most countries, although once it was the norm. In families, the promise of the Lord Jesus to be present with the two or three gathered together can be realised, as it has often been in times of persecution.

It is our conviction that family worship is an essential element of local Church gathering. Well established family worship under the guidance of Church leadership is the best safeguard against the encroachment of the State in times of crisis. It is our prayer that the *Help,* and *Simply Psalms for Singing*, may encourage the use of the Psalms in worship, and particularly their recovery in family and personal worship.

Advertisement:

1. A Help for using the Psalms in Personal and Family Worship

The *Help* calendarises the whole book of Psalms, and provides one-page devotional and expository notes for each day of the year.

Many Christians today do not know where to start in singing the Psalms, and are unaware of the resources that are available. The *Help* meets that need.

The Book answers questions 'Who should sing Psalms?'; 'Why should we sing the Psalms?'; 'When should we sing the Psalms?'; 'Where should we sing the Psalms?'; 'How should we sing the Psalms?'; 'What about the Psalms that seem to wish bad things on the enemies of Israel?'

The book's object is to encourage the use of the Psalms in personal and family worship.

Although the daily notes can simply be used devotionally, we hope that families and individuals will be encouraged by them to regain the habit of singing the Psalms.

There are 'Thinking Points' for the daily portions that can be used to help participation in family worship, or to give individuals further things to consider.

Advertisement:

2. Simply Psalms for Singing:
A translation for singing arranged in daily portions

This is a new translation of the Psalms for singing.

With its sister book *(A Help for using the Psalms in Personal and Family Worship)* it enables the singing of the complete Book of Psalms in a year. It is divided into the same 365 portions as the *Help*.

It uses a single metre throughout, so that individuals and families can easily sing without requiring musical ability.

It is produced in blank verse without the restriction that rhyme imposes on translation.

It attempts to stay as close as possible to the inspired Hebrew words, whilst clearly expressing the meaning.

It avoids dynamic translation that simply interprets difficult lines.

It is translated from the Hebrew, with reference to a wide range of Hebrew study materials, lexicons and commentaries.

It does not attempt to reinterpret the Psalms, or to use any of the modern English versions as its basis. In its preparation, Reformation and post-Reformation translations such as the Geneva Bible, the Authorised Version, The Welsh Bible, the Dutch States Bible *(Statenvertaling)*, and Calvin's translation were constantly referred to, and regular reference was also made to the Septuagint.

We have carefully distinguished Hebrew words in the translation, such as the different words used for man and for God.

Simply Psalms for Singing and the *Help* can be used independently. The *Help* can be used with another metrical psalter. *Simply Psalms for Singing* can be used with a commentary.

Advertisement:

Simply Psalms for Singing: An Expanded Edition

This expanded edition of *Simply Psalms for Singing* has extensive footnotes and appendices.

The extra materials explain translation issues and the basis of the decisions made in this translation, as well as giving exegetical comments.

It considers key Hebrew words used in the Psalms in depth.

It is intended for serious Bible Study, and to assist anyone who leads group or family worship working through the Psalms

---

Updates on publications will be available at www.pearlpublications.co.uk.

Samples from the *Help for using the Psalms* and *Simply Psalms for Singing* are given on the next pages

Day 98

Psalm 46

He makes wars to cease

This is the first of three Psalms that describe, in order, the events that will take place at the return of the Lord Jesus. We have in this Psalm the Lord putting down all his enemies. Psalm 47 describes his coronation, and Psalm 48 the establishment of his kingdom in 'the city of the great King'.

The previous Psalm (45:3) called upon the LORD to gird on his sword. Here he acts for the deliverance of his people. He is our refuge and strength, a very present help in trouble. Encouraged by this Psalm, Luther wrote his hymn, the *Marseillaise* of the Reformation, 'A mighty fortress is our God'.

This deliverance is marked by great and manifest intervention by the LORD on behalf of his people. Its timing is when he makes wars to cease and when weapons of warfare will be destroyed - when he shall reign, and put down all his enemies (v8,9; compare Mic. 4:1-3; Rev. 11:15-18). May that day come soon!

In his last days, John Warburton[1] remarked that it is impossible to be 'still' in great trial (v10) – the Devil will take care of that!'. What is meant is, 'We must be still from helping God. He wants none of our help, neither will he have it!'

---

[1] John Warburton, *Mercies of a Covenant God*,

Sample from 'Simply Psalms for Singing: An Expanded Edition'

Day 98 **Psalm 46**

¹ God is to us our refuge and our strength:
A very present help in time of need.
² Therefore, we will not fear though earth be changed -
Though mountains be removed into the seas¹ -

³ Although their waters foam, although they roar;
Though mountains tremble at its surging tide. ╫
⁴ There is a river whose streams will make glad
The holy dwelling place² of the Most High³.

⁵ God in the midst of it: it won't be moved.
And God will help it when the morning breaks.
⁶ The nations were in tumult; kingdoms moved.
The earth did melt when he raised up his voice.

⁷ The LORD of Hosts is present with us now.
The God of Jacob. He is our high tower. ╫
⁸ Come and behold the things the LORD has done.
He has made desolations in the earth.

⁹ To earth's remotest end he makes wars cease.
He breaks the bow, and cuts the spear in two.
The chariots he burns up in the fire.
¹⁰ 'Be still and surely know that I am God!'

'Among the nations I'll be lifted up.
I will be lifted up in all the earth'.
¹¹ The LORD of Hosts is present with us now.
The God of Jacob, he is our high tower. ╫

---

¹ Literally: 'to the heart of seas'.
² Dwelling place: Hebrew plural. The holy 'dwelling places' of the Most High. In Exod. 25:9 it is the word (singular) used for the Tabernacle. It is derived from the verb šakhan - שָׁכַן, from which comes the word Shekinah (šekhînâ - שְׁכִינָה), meaning God's Divine presence that dwelt there (Exod. 25:8). Newton (7) notes four 'dwelling places' of Divine glory: the Temple, Mount Zion, the Heavenly City, and Heaven itself.
³ The Most High: Hebrew 'Elyôn - עֶלְיוֹן. See Appendix 2 - Names of God.

www.ingramcontent.com/pod-product-compliance
Lightning Source LLC
Chambersburg PA
CBHW080612300426
43661CB00144B/899